THE GIRL CODE

A Girl's Biblical System to Godliness

Life Application Devotional

TONCHELLE WARD

Copyright © 2019
"The Girl Code: A Girl's Biblical System To Godliness"
by *Tonchelle Ward*
Published by BRD Publications

The author alone, *Tonchelle Ward*, holds the rights to any and all content in this book. No parts may or should be duplicated or sold without the written permission of said author or those that said authors give contracted permission to. Some parts may be quoted or used for marketing purposes in small part and with reference to the author or publisher. All quotes are followed by their names.

CONTENTS

Foreword 1

1. Prayer: Talking To The Father 7

2. Waiting On God After You Have Prayed 14

3. Forgiveness 20

4. Know Your Role As A Woman 33

5. The Makeover 40

6. Get You A Spotter 49

7. Learning To Say No, Denying Self To Glorify God 54

8. How To Lose And Not Become Lost 63

9. Know Your Issue So You Can Be Healed 73

10. You Are Qualified To Work In God's Kingdom 80

11. When Your Emotions Don't Match Your Character 86

The Need for the Code 93

Final Word 96

FOREWORD

"The Girl Code, Loving The Me I See" ....

As women, many of us spend most of our time caring for the needs of others while neglecting who we really are. We sacrifice, give, invest and trust others while we secretly suffer to love who we are or have allowed ourselves to become as a result of life's experiences. Often times we pretend to be whole while hiding the brokenness that lies within us. We put up great defenses through sassy attitudes, harsh tongues, and feelings of entitlement. This often leads to further disappointments and self-sabotage as we become destructive to others.

We dress ourselves up, put on makeup, covering our pain to, momentarily, feel good about ourselves. Most women don't look like what we feel on the inside, but once we get home and remove all the glitz and glam, reality sets in. We are truly not the flawless or confident individuals we portray, nor are we really happy with ourselves. Many women feel alone, struggle for acceptance, and are not pleased with what we see in the mirror. This becomes an endless cycle of getting into character and not recognizing the value God has placed on the inside of us. We lay down our morals and values and compromise our spirits to fit into circles and groups that eventually break us down further through slander, greed, lack of loyalty, backbiting, jealousy, and wickedness. It is time to remove the mask of guilt, shame, hurt, pain, disappointment, and lowliness to reveal the wonder that God intended when he created you "woman".

> *Genesis 2:18 reads "And the Lord God said,*
> *It is not good that man should be alone;*
> *I will make him a help meet for him. (KJV)*

You were created to be a help meet, which is why you have the innate desire to help, but in your helping, you must understand and appreciate your own value. You were created to have dominion along with man, and not be subjected to mistreatment and disrespect. Eve was an individual in the absence of Adam. She was created with her own mind and soul. Eve's uniqueness was carefully formed by God, as she was Adam's good thing. Eve made Adam good and not the other way around.

It is my prayer that after reading and applying the biblical principles of this devotional, you will begin to love yourself according to the Word of God. "Loving The Me I See", is the motto of *The Girl Code* Women's Ministry that God has placed in me. The purpose of this ministry is to intercede on behalf of the women of God, to partner with women from various races, social and economic statuses; to teach biblical principles that will transform our minds and enable us to become who God has uniquely created us to be.

Through the teachings and sisterhood of *The Girl Code*, the lives of women are being transformed. Their minds are becoming renewed. Women are embracing who God created them to be and are truly becoming happy with themselves in the raw state. Women are removing the masks and exemplifying characteristics of God at home, work, and in the community. Women of *The Girl Code* are realizing their value and are no longer willing to compromise themselves because happiness and joy truly lie within. Women are realizing their wonder and identifying the jewel God created them to be. Women are now presenting their bodies as living sacrifices to God and no longer using it as a tool. Remember, precious stones can't be handled by everyone.

Psalm 139:14 reads, "I will praise you because I am fearfully and wonderfully made; your works are wonderful, I know that full well." (NIV)

The Girl Code Women's Ministry does not compete! We collaborate as a sisterhood in the Kingdom of God. We recognize that each one of us is unique, but together we are a mighty force.

The focus of this devotional is solely about self-evaluation and becoming God's masterpiece in your own mind. You believe what you perceive. After reading and applying the principles in this devotional you will be able to effectively help others while loving yourself. You will also be complete within yourself to no longer feel the need to hide your brokenness, as it will no longer exist. You should begin to walk in your freedom in Christ.

John 8:36 reads "If the Son therefore shall make you free, ye shall be free indeed" (KJV)

After applying these biblical principles to your daily life, you should be able to: give empathy and not sympathy, operate in the joy of the Lord, transform your mind so that your character will transform, and truly begin to love yourself. Knowing the Word of God is not enough, you must apply it! Loving yourself allows you to be confident, but not cocky. When you truly love yourself, you can genuinely smile in the mirror at the woman who never existed or who has been dormant for too long. Loving yourself allows you to look adversity in the face and declare that victory is mine because I was created to conquer. Loving yourself allows you to walk away from anything that threatens your peace and does not recognize your worth.

The chapters (The Code) of this book were strategically arranged to allow you to begin removing the layers that prevent you from loving yourself. Spiritual transformation is an internal process and with God's grace, you can change, if you are ready to put in the work. I encourage you to follow the system of the code as presented as there may be a revelation into areas you did not know existed.

Transform Your Mind and Your Character Will Transform!

Transformed:

Romans 12:2 reads

"Don't copy the behavior and customs of this world, but let God transform you into a new person by changing the way you think. Then you will learn to know God's will for you, which is good and pleasing and perfect". (NLT)

"And do not be conformed to this world, but be transformed by the renewing of your mind, so that you may prove what the will of God is, that which is good and acceptable and perfect." (KJV)

CHAPTER 1

PRAYER: TALKING TO THE FATHER

Pray for Understanding
Daily Quote:
"Prayer Changes Things"

Message:

Transformation begins with understanding how to communicate with God. Prayer is our way to communicate with God, but we must remember that communication includes both speaking and listening. We must make our requests known to God and then listen for his response. We will begin the process of transformation by exploring the Model Prayer and how to effectively communicate with God. The Model Prayer is as follows:

Matthew 6:9-15(KJV)

Our Father which art in heaven
Hallowed be thy name.
Thy kingdom come.
Thy will be done

In earth, as it is in heaven.
Give us this day our daily bread.
And forgive us our debts, as we forgive our debtors.
And Lead us not into temptation, but deliver us from evil:
For thine is the kingdom, and the power and the glory, forever.
Amen

Prayer has many postures for example: standing with arms stretched out with palms open, outstretched arms with hands cupped, sitting, kneeling, and lying down prostrate.

Standing with arms stretched out: places you in the position to receive. It is simply opening yourself up to God to receive what he has for you. Waiting on the open heaven to shower down its blessings.

Sitting: places you in a position of authority. Sitting is synonymous with sitting at the right hand of the Father. You belong to him and he belongs to you.

Kneeling: expresses honor and true humility. Kneeling in prayer signifies that you acknowledge the sovereignty of God.

Lying prostate: (face down to the floor with arms and legs stretched out) speaks to totally surrendering yourself to God. You give all of you to him and relinquish all control to him. None of you and all of him!

Regardless of the chosen posture, the key is humility. Always go before God in prayer with true humility. Your heart lifted up to him trusting and believing that he hears you. You can say a prayer anywhere and at all times, but sometimes you must steal away to a private place where it's just you and The Father. Jesus often removed himself from the people to pray and spend time alone with God.

The Model Prayer is not all-inclusive because we know that prayer is from the heart. This Prayer gives the basis for how prayer should be constructed. If you can't say anything else, say The Model Prayer with a sincere heart and talk to your Father daily. Use your own words and voice because he knows you as his own child.

Luke 11 teaches us Jesus had just prayed in a certain place and one of his disciples asked him to teach us how to pray. Jesus said unto them when you pray say...... (What we know as the Lord's Prayer, which is actually the model prayer because this was for the disciples to use).

Do you find it ironic that Jesus didn't teach them what to say until one of them asked him? This disciple wanted to be able to pray on his own. Jesus had set an example! I can imagine Jesus saying, "I'm glad you asked!" Sometimes God holds up on his goodness just waiting on us to ask him. Are you setting a prayer example with the people who are walking with you daily? As women of God, we should have our own prayer life and start asking people to "pray with us" because we are already going to the Father on our own. It is time out for simply saying "pray for me"! Become a Woman of God and not just another woman who knows of God.

The Model Prayer Matthew 6:9-15

"Our Father which art in heaven," Acknowledges who we are praying to and shows an intimate connection because we are calling on "Our

Father." Calling on "Our Father" acknowledges we know him personally and he knows us. Using the word "Our" is also showing that we are not selfish and we are acknowledging we belong to him collectively. It also shows I recognize I am not his only child. I also have some siblings in the kingdom.

"Which art in Heaven," is simply saying I know where you are God? You are not lost. If I need you, I know where to find you. I'm lifting my voice and my heart to you.

"Hallowed be thy name," is showing our Father we esteem his name as Holy. We are first showing honor to Him before we go any further. His name is like no other! We are showing him that we worship and adore Him.

"Thy kingdom come thy will be done," is asking God to allow the kingdom he has prepared for you to come. You are seeking him to allow you to live under his kingdom. Lord give me your best right now, have your way.

"On earth as it is in heaven," is asking God for the joy and peace which is in heaven to come to you on earth. You are asking for him to open up the heavens and shower down upon you.

"Give us this day our daily bread" is the first line of specifically asking for something personal, but once again this line is not selfish. You are saying give "us." You are interceding on behalf of others. "This day" signifies you are saying right now at this very moment supply an immediate need (food, shelter, and clothing whatever we need to survive.

The daily bread here represents your sustenance. Father, give us the manna from on High.

"Forgive us our debt as we forgive our debtors" another account **"Forgive us our trespasses as we forgive those who trespass against us"** This is such a POWERFUL statement!!!!! It is circumstantial and places some stipulations on us. "WE MUST FORGIVE FIRST!" We are seeking forgiveness from God, but not until we forgive others. Here we are asking God to forgive what we have done wrong, but Lord we know we must extend that same forgiveness to the ones who have wronged us. When we say these words we are calling God to examine our behaviors and grudges towards others as he forgives us. We can't ask God to do for us what we aren't willing to do for others. So, if we aren't willing to forgive others then we forfeit our forgiveness. This is forgiving the apology you never received. Forgiving the debtor of the money you never received back. Forgiving the friend/family who betrayed you, lied on you, etc. We must forgive first!

"And lead us not into temptation, but deliver us from evil" we are seeking God's protection. We are asking him to guide us when we are tempted. We want him to be in control and not allow us to fall into sin. We are saying Lord, be our way out. He always gives us a way out, but do we take it? We are saying, turn us away from temptation. As we say, "but deliver us from evil", we are simply asking for a hedge of protection. Evil will come but free us from it. Don't allow us to become devoured by evil. Don't allow Satan to win and make us lose focus on you.

"For thine is the kingdom, the power and the glory forever. Amen," is a doxology (a liturgical expression of praise to God). It appears in the model prayer written in Matthew, but not in Luke. However, here we are praising God and letting Him know that it is all about Him. For thine is the kingdom means, God I am acknowledging everything belongs to you. "The power and the glory," is solidifying the adoration and praise to God. We are saying God has the power and deserves the glory. We are telling God we know who he is and what he possesses. Just as we opened our prayer with honor and praise, we close our prayer with honor and praise. We are telling God that He reigns forever and everything is done unto him. When we say "Amen", we are saying "I believe!" Saying Amen signifies we believe that everything we have just communicated to Our Father God, will happen.

Remember, as you pray daily you are free to talk to the Father as needed, according to your relationship with him.

Just as the game Pac-man is played, we go through life eating the dots which symbolize our different systems (home, school, work, family, community, etc.). The ghosts are like the enemy trying to kill and destroy you before you finish your course. However, the game changes when Pac-man eats the power pellet. This is an indication of how we are when we activate the power of prayer. When your power becomes activated, through prayer, you are in control and the enemy flees from you. You are now in a position of power to destroy those enemies and send them back to the pit of hell. There will always be more of the enemy's imps than you but activate your prayer power and they will flee.

LIFE APPLICATION CHAPTER 1

1. Pray daily; you must have a prayer life
2. Believe in the power of your prayers
3. Pray and listen for God to communicate his will to you
4. Speak your desires clearly to God and do not mimic the prayers of others

> *Proverbs 16:3 reads "Commit to the Lord whatever you do, and he will establish your plans."*

Personal Goal (Examine yourself and write down what you plan to do differently regarding prayer.)

_____
_____
_____
_____
_____
_____
_____
_____
_____
_____
_____
_____
_____

CHAPTER 2

WAITING ON GOD AFTER YOU HAVE PRAYED

Pray for Understanding
Daily Quote:
"Delayed is not a denied; wait on God!"

Message:

"What to do during the time out; the period after you have prayed?"

Psalm 27:14 (KJV) "Wait for the Lord; be of good courage, and he shall strengthen thine heart, wait, I say, on the Lord."

Most of us are familiar with the games of basketball and football. During the game, each team is given a predetermined number of time outs to be utilized at their discretion when they need a break or a period to refocus and strategize their next move. During the time out the players are generally in a resting state while receiving specific instructions from their coach. The coach has considered all possible outcomes, evaluated the strengths and weaknesses of the opponents, and has devised a specific plan to yield a victory.

This is what happens in life when we go to God in prayer and cry out to him with our heart. We then enter into the time out period. The time out requires us to focus on God and rest our cares upon him. We must yield to his way. During the time out, God has assessed our situation and he knows what is best for us to yield the best results. What is best may mean taking our hands off the ball and passing it! It may mean delaying the play until time almost runs out and then making a strategic move with the opponent not having time for another play. What is best, if improperly executed, may still result in a loss but we stayed in the game. Therefore, the play after the time out must be executed to perfection! No room for errors.

In the game of life, we must trust God during the waiting/time out period. It is the period after the prayer called the "process." We have four stages in the game of life PLAN, PRAYER, PROCESS, AND PURPOSE.

> *Jeremiah 29:11 (KJV) declares, "For I know the thoughts that I think toward you, saith the Lord, thoughts of peace, and not of evil, to give you an expected end."*

God knows the "plan" he has for us. As we go to him in "prayer" for directions and guidance the "process" is the work or sometimes the lack of work. The "purpose" for our lives is what we find after we have surrendered to God.

If you are playing a tough game of life right now, get the referee's (God's) attention through prayer. He controls the game and has the final say! Then go on the sideline and allow the coach (Jesus) to give you the next move. Pay attention during the time out so you can hear God's voice clearly. This is not the time to be distracted by the crowd. The next move should be under the guidance of the Holy Spirit and may determine the overall fate of the game! Remember, the time out never ends the game. It pauses the clock to allow for a new strategy.

Psalm 69:1:3 (KJV) "Save me, O God; for the waters are come in unto my soul. I sink in deep mire, where there is no standing: I am come into deep waters, where the floods overflow me. I am weary of my crying: my throat is dried: mine eyes fail while I wait for my God."

This Psalm written by David speaks of being overwhelmed by struggles, not just minor struggles, but the ones that overtake you. The struggles which lead you to think you are drowning in the deep with no escape. David speaks of crying out to the point which caused his throat to become dry and he had nothing more physically to give to his sorrows/trials while he waits on God. David knew God was his refuge so he had to have faith. What is our course of action during the time out? It is quite simple, Have FAITH!!!

We must have faith God is working things out even when we cannot see a way. During the time out we are at rest listening to the voice of God and believing in what he said he would do. It is the only way. The next play is the one which wins the game. Activated faith after the time out is the play which yields the victory. The **faith play** may not be the expected outcome of the opponent, but it is the one that was projected by God for his children. Satan cannot win when it comes to God. Activated faith is synonymous to the half-court shot at the buzzer. It is the shot that even surprises the player when it goes in! Activated faith is like the interception in the end zone with no seconds left on the clock. Activate your faith while waiting on God and celebrate the victory. We always win through Christ!!!! Spoiler alert, **we won before the game began!!!!** During the time out listen to the play and get back in the game of life with FAITH! You cannot win without it.

Isaiah 40:31(KJV) (my favorite scripture) says, "But they that wait on the Lord shall renew their strength; they shall mount up with wings as eagles; they shall run, and not be weary and they shall walk, and not faint."

This passage of scripture speaks to the result of waiting on God. As we cry out to God in prayer we should use our faith and have an expectation of God's blessings upon our lives. Isaiah 40:31 tells us that while waiting on the Lord we gain strength. No matter what we are going through, we will encounter that moment when we are knocked so far down the only place to go is up! We somehow gain the strength to get up again. When we are weak God is our strength.

As we are waiting on God we must view ourselves as a powerful eagle who soars through the sky. We should be carefree as we watch God work things out on our behalf. Remember, the eagle does not have to overwork itself by constantly flapping its wings. It simply takes flight, flaps its powerful wings, and rides the wind (soaring). This is pure confidence in the success of the journey. This is the expected end! The strength and peace we should possess while we are waiting on God. Soar through the challenges of life as the eagle; strong, powerful, confident and in control.

This scripture exemplifies more strength by stating that while waiting on God we must run and not get weary. Stay on the course. Don't stop moving. While waiting on God we should have the strength to keep running and not get tired. The key is to run the race at our own pace. God knows you and what you can endure. Hold true to the promises of God for you!! ***Your problem, your promise!*** You can't seek someone else's promise if you aren't willing to take on their problem(s).

LIFE APPLICATION CHAPTER 2

1. Pray to God and wait for his response
2. Listen carefully to his instructions because the outcome for your life depends on it
3. Activate your faith (FAITH is an acronym, FORGET ALL I TRUST HIM)
4. Get ready to win

> *Proverbs 16:3 (KJV) "Commit to the Lord whatever you do, and he will establish your plans."*

Personal Goal (Examine yourself and write down what you plan to do differently regarding waiting on God.)

_____
_____
_____
_____
_____
_____
_____
_____
_____
_____
_____

CHAPTER 3

FORGIVENESS

Pray for Understanding
Daily Quote:
"Forgiveness is Freedom"

Message:

Forgiveness; SELF, GOD, OTHERS, ASKING OTHERS TO FORGIVE YOU

Forgiving Self:

1 John 1:9 (KJV) If we confess our sins, he is faithful and just to forgive us our sins, and to cleanse us from all unrighteousness.

We develop morals and values from our family, environment and those people with whom we interact with regularly. We may find ourselves getting good advice, bad advice, and some advice we need to forget and never use or repeat! We are forced to tap into our own value system, including, consciousness, and situational awareness to make decisions we think are best at the given time. We consider the facts, assess possible outcomes, add a little judgment and speculation, and come up with a decision on how we will handle the presented problem. Sometimes we make good decisions and have favorable results and other times we make poor decisions. Regardless of the decision, we must live with the consequences of our actions. There will come a point in our lives when we will hear the phrase, "experience is the best teacher" and this is so true!

As we experience life, at some point we find ourselves dealing with the consequences of OUR poor decisions. We make countless mistakes and are constantly holding on for God's grace and mercy. Although to err is human, wisdom is not making the same mistake twice. At some point, we realize that we have caused our own problem(s) and it is time to stop blaming others and learn to forgive ourselves.

As women, BE HONEST, we trust too much (the signs were there but we ignored them). We give too much (they did not honor the previous arrangement(s), but we gave again). We sacrifice too much (they would not do it for us, but oh well). We give up too much (putting our wants and needs secondary to try and make him/her happy) all for the sake of love and the betterment of others. We hear the voice of reason telling us that we should not do it (God gives us an out), but we do it anyway. Then, we spend years feeling down on ourselves because we feel as if we should have done things differently to have a different outcome. We feel ashamed, betrayed, and let down.

It is time for us to forgive ourselves. It is time to confess your sins and mistakes to God, ask for forgiveness, and most importantly FORGIVE YOURSELF! Yes, you said the wrong thing at the wrong time. Yes, you made the wrong decision and cannot undo the outcome. Yes, you made a mistake, but now you know better. Experience has taught you what you will and will not accept. Yes, you gave too much, but now you know to give within reason and when giving hurts you, stop! Yes, you have wasted precious time, your resources, and put yourself in financial bondage, but now you know what it means to be abased and how to abound.

Philippians 4:12 (KJV) "I know both how to be abased, and I know how to abound; every where and in all things I am instructed both to be full and to be hungry, both to abound and to suffer need."

If you had not pushed the limits, then you would not have clear boundaries.

Look in the mirror and say to yourself, "Girl, you made a mistake, but I love you. I forgive you, lesson learned and now it is time to move on!" Say, "I am wiser, I am stronger and I am no longer bound!" Free yourself from the bondage of shame, doubt, and pity. Acknowledge that you have made the wrong choice, and work on another plan. What if you dreamed of that college degree and never started or did not finish? If you are reading this, your fresh start is now! Now that you have acknowledged it give it to God and get ready for a transformation. You did it your way, now do it God's way. In Christ, you are no longer the same and are more than a conqueror.

Romans 8:37 (KJV) "Nay, in all these things we are more than conquerors through him that loved us"

Pick up your head, gain your stride, and walk into your freedom. Forgive yourself! You know better, now do better. God has given you another chance. Seek God for guidance, obey his instructions, and wait for a life-changing answer.

Forgiving God: This one right here requires one to assess the true meaning of trust in God when the outcome breaks your heart and weakens your faith. There are times in our life when we need to encourage others. We find it so easy to pull out those familiar religious clichés like, "God won't put more on you than you can bear." "God's will shall be done." "Give it to God and leave it there. Here is the big one, "If you have faith the size of a mustard seed you can move mountains (paraphrase)." All of these are correct and makes a believer proud to encourage someone in a struggle. These words are safe to encourage others and they sound good, but what do they really mean when you are the one hurting?

What happens when you do your best and a loved one still dies, a marriage still ends, a child still gets tried by life circumstances, a home is still foreclosed, a business still fails, or promotion is never granted? You may not even feel like praying. You feel like just when you are finally doing things according to the Word, all hell is breaking loose. Constant life struggles cause you to become weary. You may even get to a point where your faith is tested and you are tempted to give up on doing the right thing. You may even start thinking; "I am going to give up on this Christian living, start wilding out, and doing me because the sinner man always looks happy and happiness is what I desire!" (Read Psalm 73).

You become angry with God! You trust him and yet you feel betrayed. You know the things to say to others, but you cannot muster the strength to say them to yourself! Losing trust in someone is not easy to regain, but what happens when we begin to lose trust in God and what he has promised you? It is ironic during the lowest point in our lives we run across someone going through a struggle and we still have to pull out the trusty cliché even while we have diminished faith. This is when God is testing us and true ministry is manifested. Remember, even as Jesus was on the cross he cared for his mother and the two thieves on his sides. The ability to minister to others while wounded ourselves shows God that you can be trusted and it draws you closer to him.

Sometimes we have to forgive God for allowing our hearts to break. It is easy to get angry with God when what we wanted is delayed, or denied. God sometimes breaks our heart to protect us. He sees what we cannot see and he knows what we do not know.

When we pray for peace, healing, comfort, and joy we don't know how he will give it! It is time to forgive God for breaking your heart and trust that he knows what is best for you. He may have protected you because what was to come next you could not handle. Repent for doubting him and losing faith when life happened. Free yourself from the bondage of not basking in his glory because of your unbelief. God never fails and he has an expected end for you. Trust God but most importantly trust the process. Forgive God for how he chose to protect you. Parents must sometimes break their children's hearts to protect them. FORGIVE GOD because you do not know why he did it, but just know that it was for your good. He cares for you!

Forgiving Others:

Matthew 18:21-22 (NIV) Then Peter came to Jesus and asked, "Lord, how many times shall I forgive my brother or sister who sins against me? Up to seven times?" Jesus answered, I tell you, not seven times, but seventy-seven times.

Forgiving others is one of the hardest things to do sometimes. We tend to become stagnated in our hurt. We allow our thoughts of the offense to prevent us from totally healing, thus making it impossible to forgive the offender.

Reflecting on our lesson of the model prayer we are to constantly pray to God *"forgive us our debts as we forgive our debtors"*. This is a conditional statement in which our forgiveness from God happens as we forgive others. We are simply saying, "Lord show me the forgiveness I show to others." When was the last time you asked God for forgiveness for something wrong that you had done? Did you expect forgiveness? What if he does not grant it because you have not forgiven others?

Our focus scripture says we are to forgive others seventy-seven times which means an endless number of times. If someone asks for forgiveness, then we are to show God's love and mercy and forgive them. We often hear, "I may forgive, but I won't forget!" True forgiving is not forgetting the offense but forgetting the need to get back or bring it up again. Forgiving is removing the need to use the offense as ammunition in the future. No firing back!

Very rarely do people set out to intentionally hurt us. We get hurt in the process of their selfishness, need for pleasure, or lack of consideration towards us. We are not the target, but we are hurt by their decision(s). We become the casualty! Like being struck as the innocent bystander. Although the intent was not there, the hurt/pain/consequence is real and cannot be undone. Walk in freedom and forgive others. We can no longer be enslaved by being unforgiving to others and risk being unforgiven by God. Is someone else worth crippling how God shows mercy to you?

Forgive your parents who were uneducated and made poor life decisions which caused undue hardship to your mental state and emotional stability. It planted a seed of instability which led to you not trusting others. Now you struggle in relationships because you question genuine love. You unconsciously believe if the ones who should love and protect you failed to do their jobs properly, then it is impossible for someone else to truly love you. *Free yourself and forgive your parent(s).*

Forgive your children who went against all the morals and values you tried to instill in them by choosing a life which introduced them to the same problems you prayed and labored against. The same children you reared have become the teens and adults you rallied against, but they are yours and you love them. Keep praying, you have done your best.

Proverbs 22:6. (KJV) "Train up a child in the way he should go: and when he is old, he will not depart from it."

Free yourself and forgive your children.
Forgive that friend in whom you confided and later learned your business was not kept in their heart but it left their lips. Now you know better. Sometimes your business is discussed with others, yet it does not mean

they do not care or had ill intent. Maybe you were discussed because they care and could not handle the information you shared with them. What if they are secretly seeking advice or assistance with helping you?

The real problem is the person that they told could not be trusted, otherwise, how would you have known? Being discussed is not always mess. It is based on intent. Everyone cannot handle your reality! Know your circle and know what you can share with whom. Be honest, you too have shared someone's business before. If someone starts the dialogue with "don't tell anybody" or "this is between us" it is because they believe that telling someone's business to another is common. Be suspicious of those who begin with a disclaimer as they proceed to tell you another person's business. If someone speaks your truth, don't get angry. Your truth is your truth. Tell your problems to God and you will not hear it again.

> *1 Peter 5:7. (NLT) "Give all your worries and cares to God, for he cares for you."*

Free yourself and forgive your friend.
Forgive the person(s) you love or have loved and trusted who broke your heart countless times, through lies, deception, abuse (verbal and physical) and infidelity. Those are selfish actions which had nothing to do with you. Self-gratification was more important than their loyalty to you. Trust me, it was not about you!!! You were the casualty! Maybe it is a generational curse and they are fighting internal battles which have nothing to do with you.

What if they will never do things differently because they like what they do and do not want to stop? What if they do not know how to love you? What if they do not love themselves? There is nothing you could have done to result in a different outcome. They are not living their truth. Therefore, lying and deceit have become natural to them. What if they are living a lie because of you? They do not want you to see the real them. If you knew their truths, you would not love them based on their secret struggles.

Free yourself and forgive the one who hurt you.
Some people do not have the coping mechanisms to deal with life's challenges, so they develop defense mechanisms. Commonly used defense mechanisms are **denial** (refusing to accept the reality of a painful event; **projection** (attributing one's own unacceptable thoughts, feelings and motives to another person; **sublimation** (satisfying an inappropriate impulse with a more socially acceptable behavior and **displacement** (unconsciously discharging repressed feelings or emotions on to objects/people less threatening. Some people defend themselves from hurt and pain by masking it with other people and behaviors. You became the sacrifice for their struggle. It is time to forgive others so God can forgive you and true healing can begin. It is time to show God that you deserve his mercy because you know how to show mercy towards others.

> *Matthew 5:16 (KJV) "Let your light so shine before men,*
> *that they may see your good works and glorify your*
> *Father which is in heaven."*

Those incidents in which you never received an apology, forgive those too! Be like Joseph who had to forgive his brothers who hated him and threw him in the pit. The pit placed him in a position to get to the palace. Joseph held onto the promises of God. *(Read Genesis 37 – 50)*. If a person hurts you and never apologizes you must forgive them anyway. If they could not make an unselfish decision that ultimately hurt you, then what makes you believe they will put themselves to the side and sincerely apologize? Some may even call themselves apologizing by trying to justify their wrong actions as something you made them do. Just accept THEY MAY NOT KNOW HOW TO APOLOGIZE OR WHAT TO SAY! Forgive them for not knowing how they made you feel.

Free yourself and forgive others.

Asking others to forgive you!

> *Matthew 19:12 (KJV) "Who can understand his errors? cleanse thou me from secret faults."*

It is so easy for us to see the faults in others and readily acknowledge when someone has done us wrong, but can we accept knowing we have done wrong to others. Sometimes we must humble ourselves and ask someone to forgive us. This one can be tough but it may be necessary. Women of God, I encourage you to make the first move!

If you knowingly offend someone you must humbly go to that person and ask for forgiveness. Remember, you are asking for forgiveness because you offended them. You are not agreeing or disagreeing with the need to be right in the matter.

Acknowledging you are right or wrong may gain personal satisfaction, but it does not negate the offense to another. Before my transformation, I had always taken the position, if I said it I meant it! I am sorry if it hurt your feelings but I am not sorry for what I said. Now, through Christ, I no longer apologize in that manner. *Therefore, if any man be in Christ, he is new (KJV)* Now, I apologize for my role in the matter and move on.

If someone expresses to you that you have offended them by your actions, words, gestures, deeds, or lack of any of the above be willing to accept the fact that you have offended them and apologize. There is no need at this point to fight for justification of why you acted in the manner you did. Just apologize for your part and free yourself. You may have heard that every action brings a reaction, but the reaction can sometimes be offensive and you will be held accountable for it by God.

Furthermore, there are times when you are secretly at fault. You do things to others and may not realize the magnitude of what you have done and how they were impacted. You may have done or said something when that person was at a fragile point in life and your actions were taken offensively. If the offense is never expressed you may spend the rest of your life not knowing why you lost a connection with someone dear to you. If this is the case, it is time to swallow your pride and ask for their forgiveness. Say, if I have offended you in any way, I apologize.

Side note: AN APOLOGY MAY NOT BE ACCEPTED, (they have that right)! You have done your part, *free yourself.*

The simple gesture of asking for forgiveness may erase a longtime misunderstanding. Asking someone to forgive you frees you from bondage and places the burden on them to accept. Remember, you can only control your own actions. Take control of you and ask for forgiveness. It may be the difference between the life and death of a relationship. When asking for forgiveness do not bring up the details of the incident, just apologize for your actions and move on. It is the difference of opinion that broke the connection in the first place so there is no need to rehash the incident. You are seeking freedom so ask for forgiveness whether YOU feel you are right or wrong. DON'T JUSTIFY YOUR POSITION in the matter. Ask for forgiveness and free yourself. Forgiveness is deliverance.

LIFE APPLICATION CHAPTER 3

1. Pray to God and ask him to forgive you for not forgiving others
2. Pray for a forgiving heart
3. Identify people and situations that you need to forgive
4. Ask others to forgive you

Proverbs 16:3 "Commit to the Lord whatever you do, and he will establish your plans."

Personal Goal (Examine yourself and write down what you plan to do differently regarding forgiveness.)

_____
_____
_____
_____
_____
_____
_____
_____
_____
_____
_____
_____

CHAPTER 4

KNOW YOUR ROLE AS A WOMAN

Pray for Understanding
Daily Quote:
"I am Necessary and Man's Good Thing!"

Message:

Psalm 139:14-15 (KJV) "I will praise thee; for I am fearfully and wonderfully made: marvelous are thy works; and that my soul knoweth right well. My substance was not hid from thee, when I was made in secret, and curiously wrought in the lowest parts of the earth."

In Psalm 139, David is speaking his heart to God. David is telling God he understands that God never leaves him no matter where he goes. He is also confessing that God knows everything about him and still chooses to be with him always. David acknowledges to God, he knew him in the **secret of the womb** and he was made wonderfully complex. Although David confesses these things in the Psalm, they are still applicable to us today. God made us, he knows all about us and he never leaves us.

This is great news!

The Role: At the knowledge of conception, a woman begins to bond with the unborn child. The anticipation of the delivery and gender begins to heighten. Some women desire to have girls while others want boys. After giving birth, parents unconsciously begin to prepare the young child for gender roles. Little girls are reared to be responsible wives and mothers with baby dolls, kitchen sets, playing school as teachers and caring for the sick as nurses. Little girls are taught to take care of the home and care for and nurture others. On the contrary, little boys are often reared as thrill seekers who constantly need supervision for their own protection. They are given basketballs, footballs, big trucks, and toy guns. Girls are not naturally groomed to be thrill seekers and boys are not naturally groomed to be husbands and fathers.

I acknowledge there are exceptions to these norms in some families. Some families do not define roles by societal norms, but this speaks to the majority. Thus, the ideology of the roles! Societal norms reinforce a girl's role is to give of herself to others and the boy's role is to be self-contained. This standard is set at an early age and is sometimes chiseled into our minds to the point of destruction.

The Creation: The Book of Genesis begins with the miraculous work of God creating the heavens, earth, and man. God spoke and formed the world and life into existence in six days then on the seventh day he rested. As we study Genesis, we see the creation was not completed and God did not rest until he made man in his image. Before day six, everything God made was very good. **Eden was good in all its likeness.** However, after the creation of man, God said for the first time that something was not good. The state of Adam's being was not good.

God And The Helpmeet:

> *Genesis 2:18 (KJV) "God said, it is not good for man to be alone, I will make him a helpmeet "fit for him".*

You will be his strength in times of weakness. You will fill his voids. When he is not good at something you will be and vice versa. The fit is not simply fulfilling the desires of his flesh, for that can easily lead to falling into sin. The flesh can be temporarily satisfied by many but the spirit gets fulfilled through God. The woman created for him will be able to pray him through situations. The woman of God created for him will challenge the King in him. Eve challenged the King in Adam when she was deceived. Imagine the outcome if Adam had taken his rightful position in a perfect Eden and stood on the instructions of God.

The instructions were given to Adam to not eat of the fruit but he did not maintain his position. Women, you must be careful who you allow to get close to you and speak into your spirit. You could be destroying your destiny as the helpmeet. Satan met with the woman because she is the carrier of the seed and giver of life. The woman had great influence. How are you using your influence? Whose voice are you listening to?

The helpmeet was created to fulfill several roles in the life of a man and without a woman **fit for him,** God said, "man is not good." A girlfriend or boyfriend is the pre-requisite to marriage, but it is not the order of a spiritual life. Girlfriends can do well and fulfill some tasks, but a wife brings favor!

Wife, Good Thing And Favor: The bible states, a man who finds a wife finds a good thing and obtains favor with the Lord. A man of God uses his discernment to find the missing part of him. The <u>**natural missing link to his chain.**</u> When she is found there should be something uniquely happening on the inside of him. Man was not good alone, but God created the "good thing for him".

Genesis 2:21 says, "And the Lord caused a deep sleep to fall upon Adam, and he slept: and he took one of a rib and closed up the flesh instead thereof " See, the closing of the flesh was to protect his inner being/his spirit and not allow what does not fit to enter into man.

Why The Rib: The ribs give support to the expansion and contraction of the thoracic cavity. During inhalation, the rib cage expands as rib muscles contract. During exhalation, the rib cage gets smaller as rib muscles relax. As the rib, when the man takes in problems on the job, lack of resources, and low self-esteem we are to rise up and expand. We are to get bigger when he is taking in the troubles of this world. Women, you must be what he needs. How many of us know this must happen in the absence of proper communication?

As the man exhales (breathes out) he blows off frustration and releases the plan from God. As the rib, we are to get smaller and retreat back. He must be allowed to get it out. Our role is to allow for exhalation without disrupting the process. If we get smaller during inhalation we may cause damage to the heart and lungs. If we expand during exhalation we might allow too much out. The flow of this process must be in precision to minimize risks and damage to the body.

The ribs also give shape and support to the chest. It provides a strong framework onto which the muscles of the shoulder girdle, chest, upper abdomen, and back can attach. According to God's plan, not man, (remember God caused Adam to sleep when he took the rib), the woman gives support and shape to man. He did not ask for Adam's opinion on what he liked or how he wanted her. He gave him what he needed. Adam did not have anything to do with what God knew he needed. God created the woman fit for him. The role of the woman is to shape and support the man. As a man roams to discover his true identity and purpose, being the thrill seeker, his life does not take its true shape and gain support until he discerns the woman God has fit for him. She may not be easy, but she will serve is spirit man.

The ribs form a protective cage around the heart and the lungs, protecting them from physical damage from outside. The woman is the protector of life. She protects her children and her husband in prayer and deeds. She protects the man's heart because whatever controls the heart controls him. As the rib, she also protects his lungs which ironically protects his life. A wife will go to war for her husband against anything and anybody who rises up against him. The wife sits in the bay and tries to be dignified and in order, but when things get rough she is on the side as a partner in WWE wrestling match. She is waiting like oooooooohhhh tag me in! If you have ever watched wrestling, when the fresh partner comes in things are about to change!

However, as strong as the rib may be sometimes it gets broken. After suffering blunt force sometimes a woman is broken, just like a rib. When a rib is broken, it repairs itself from within the body. A broken rib only needs to be protected, but within days of the break, it begins to heal itself and will be restored. When a rib is broken there is swelling and pain. Coughing, sneezing, or breathing deeply can cause terrible pain. When a woman is broken the function of the man and the home, experience terrible pain.

There is a huge difference between a broken rib and a jagged rib. When a rib is jagged, it can damage major blood vessels and internal organs. This means the break is raggedy, ripping has occurred and mending is not so easy. A jagged rib must be removed (divorce) because it can cause damage to the very organs it was designed to protect. Jagged ribs could puncture the heart, lungs and take life. This is true for the woman as well. A jagged woman is dangerous! It is far better to break a woman and let her heal than to leave her jagged!

The rib fit for a man will fight to protect his heart, life, support him when he is weak, and challenge the King in him so he can be his best self in the Kingdom. She will see his true nakedness and shame (the parts he hides from others) and will hang in there after the break.

You are the rib! Your role is to help not hurt. Know who you are and who God created you to be. If you get broken, retreat to your private place, wrap yourself in the arms of Jesus and begin to heal yourself.

LIFE APPLICATION CHAPTER 4

1. Pray to God to acknowledge your role as a woman
2. Assess yourself to see if you are operating according to God's plan for a woman
3. Think about what type of rib are you right now

Proverbs 16:3 "Commit to the Lord whatever you do, and he will establish your plans."

Personal Goal (Examine yourself and write down what you plan to do differently regarding operating in your role as God intended.)

_____
_____
_____
_____
_____
_____
_____
_____
_____
_____
_____
_____
_____
_____

CHAPTER 5

THE MAKEOVER

Pray for Understanding
Daily Quote:
"Lord, I need a makeover"

Message:

Psalm 139:14 (KJV) "I will praise thee; for I am fearfully and wonderfully made: marvelous are thy works; and that my soul knoweth right well."

In Psalm 139, David speaks of God as all knowing, everywhere at the same time, and having all power. God knows each one of us in an intimate way. He is with us at ALL times and has power over our lives. We cannot hide from God.

Have you ever stood in line at a grocery store and looked at the women featured on magazine covers? You will notice that each cover is unique while sharing the same rack with all the others. Each magazine displays the title of the magazine and usually a beautiful picture of the featured individual called the "Cover Girl," not the cosmetic brand but the woman on the cover. As you look carefully at each cover you will see the unique characteristics of the featured woman. There will be different races, ages, hairstyles, and body types, but one similar trait is common to each photo, each photograph expresses a personal level of confidence. Confidence is shown regardless of the personal story. The girl on the cover is owning her truth.

The cover girl is used to draw people's attention to the magazine. She has done something that makes her attractive to others. The cover girl's story is usually centrally located within the magazine because it is the featured article. Some read through until they reach that point, but others flip right to the cover girl's story and then go back and read the rest. Although the magazine has a plethora of stories and advertisements. Ultimately, it is the cover girl's story that readers want to see. Choosing the right cover girl is a way for the magazine to maximize sales and spark interest in the brand.

As women of God, we want to be able to draw people to Christ. People should be interested in how you are walking in God's presence daily. When others see you they should be intrigued by your character and want to know your story. If God had you on the cover of his magazine what would your picture say if you did not have an opportunity to speak? What stands out about you that makes others want to come to Christ? Your picture should have others saying, "What must I do to be saved?"

The cover girl must be willing to be a blank canvass for the photographer. She must be able to follow the directives of others while maintaining a smile. If the shot is not perfect she must allow editing. Image editing allows the photographer to digitally correct those imperfections of the shot to make the cover girl blemish free. Imagine God as your photographer, what does he see when he looks through the lens at you?

Like the cover girl on the magazines, you want to be the woman of God who has a story to be told. You want God to look at you and say, "Now she is the one I am choosing to draw others." She is confident, has the perfect smile, willing to be molded, and able to take directives. She is also willing to undergo some editing if it is not quite right the first time. God wants you to draw others to him but first, you must get prepared by going through the makeover.

The makeover begins with choosing the right outfit. As we go through this spiritual makeover, imagine being in a room and everyone present is wearing the same tailor-made, perfect black dress. You know, the one that makes you want to kiss yourself after you get dressed. The great thing about it being tailored made is chances are you are the only one it fits!! In the Kingdom, there is no room for comparisons. You are unique and one of a kind. So, in a world of women with everyone dressed the same, what else do you have to offer?

1 Peter 3:3-4 (KJV) "Your beauty should not come from outward adornment, such as elaborate hairstyles and the wearing of gold jewelry or fine clothes. Rather, it should be that of your inner self, the unfading beauty of a gentle and quiet spirit, which is of great worth in God's sight."

This scripture does not negate taking care of yourself, it means getting your heart right with God is more important to him than what you look like. To be an ambassador for Christ you must have a makeover.

The spiritual makeover is going to take some obedience and blinded faith because we cannot always see what God is doing with us with the human eye. You will feel different, love different, and make different choices, but the reward is going to be far greater than what the eyes can see.

The Spiritual Makeover

The Mind:

> *Isaiah 26:3 (KJV) Thou wilt keep him in perfect peace, whose mind is stayed on thee: because he trusteth in thee.*

God wants our minds stayed on him. You believe what you perceive. Sin begins with a thought and then you react. Change the way you think. Spiritual conviction happens in the mind as well. God always gives you a way out, (it is the little voice in your head) think about taking it!

The Hair:

> *2 Peter 2:20 (NIV) "If they have escaped the corruption of the world by knowing our Lord and Savior Jesus Christ and are again entangled in it and are overcome, they are worse off at the end than they were at the beginning."*

When it comes to our hair which accentuates the face, comb through to the roots to minimize tangles. Tangles represent lack of care, poor treatment and a return to confusion.

The Foundation:

1 Corinthians 3:11 (NASB) "For no man can lay a foundation other than the one which is laid, which is Jesus Christ."

Your foundation is Christ and it's already set. Your foundation is the base on which all of you is built. An unstable foundation will result in an unstable you. With the right foundation, you can only enhance what already exists.

The Eyes:

Psalm 119:18 (ESV) "Open my eyes, that I may behold wondrous things out of your law."

The eyes are used for sight. It is a shame to have sight, but lack vision. It has been stated that the eyes are the mirror to your soul. Remove the shadows of darkness and see God's marvelous light. Learn to see using your spiritual sight and not with carnal eyes. When you look in the mirror, what do you see?

The Lips:

Ephesians 4:29 (KJV) "Let no corrupt communication proceed out of your mouth, but that which is good to the use of edifying, that it may minister grace unto the hearers."

Lipstick is used to smooth and dress up the lips. Are you speaking life or death? Why dress up a trash can? Ask God to bridle your tongue so your words will not be destructive to yourself and others. Do not be a sniper in stilettos looking for the one shot to kill another with your mouth.

The Heart:

> *Matthew 5:8 (KJV) "Blessed are the pure in heart,*
> *for they shall see God."*

God wants your whole heart. He wants you to be in love with him and show that same love towards one another. Whatever has your heart has control over you. Your heart should be pure from dirt. No unclean thing should dwell in the purity of your heart.

The Hands:

> *Psalm 63:4 (NASB) "So I will bless You as long as I live;*
> *I will lift up my hands in Your name."*

Do you notice that your hands have a certain form? The fingers have a slight curve in the receiving position, but it takes some effort to open them up to give. As you exemplify God's love for another, give to others, but take some time to give to yourself. Discern what you should touch and what you should not handle. Use your hands to join in prayer, to extend in worship, and to reach out to God.

The Feet:

Psalm 119:133 (KJV) "Order my steps in thy word: and let not any iniquity have dominion over me."

God wants to order your steps, but you must surrender to him. Where he leads you must be willing to follow. Allow him to be Lord of your life. Your feet do not become new as you may have heard with the old cliché, you should just choose to go to different places. Use your feet to usher others into the presence of God.

As you strive to genuinely love yourself and be used by God, be willing to endure the makeover. You are beautiful and wonderfully made, but sin is ever present and it alters who you were created to be. God wants you to be his cover girl.

Imagine God is the writer, the angels are the editor, and the Holy Spirit is the photographer. God is looking for his cover girl. He is scanning the world, looking for the woman fit for the cover. What is so unique about you that makes you stand out from the rest? Do you simply have a pretty face, a nice body, but no spiritual sustenance? Church attendance does not provide sustenance, it comes from your lifestyle. What will be your featured story that others want to read? When others see you on the cover will they be drawn to Christ? Where is your face drawing others to?

All of us have a place in the Kingdom of God and he has different magazines that need a cover girl. Which magazine can you be chosen as the featured woman; "Wonderful," "Changed," "I'm Still," "Overcomer,"

"Grateful," "Recovered," "Delivered," or "Miracle?" You have made the cover, now what's your story? Examine yourself and own your truth.

LIFE APPLICATION CHAPTER 5

1. Pray to God and request a makeover
2. Become the blank canvas and allow God to have his way in his life
3. Be a living example of his goodness so that you may draw others to him
4. Tell your testimony to help others become delivered from sin

"Commit to the Lord whatever you do, and he will establish your plans."
Proverbs 16:3

Personal Goal (Examine yourself and write down what you plan to do differently regarding your spiritual makeover.)

_____
_____
_____
_____
_____
_____
_____
_____
_____
_____
_____

CHAPTER 6
GET YOU A SPOTTER

Pray for Understanding
Daily Quote:
"It is ok to seek help fulfilling God's assignment, even Jesus had help carrying the cross"

Message:

Luke 23:26 (NIV) "As the soldiers led him away, they seized Simon from Cyrene, who was on his way in from the country, and put the cross on him and made him carry it behind Jesus."

Every woman needs someone to help her bare the weight of the world when she can't bare it by herself. Get you a spotter! If you have ever seen weight training or competitions you will notice that there is a spotter present to help the lifter rack the weights when he/she is unable to lift them by him/herself. The spotter must be attentive to the needs of the lifter and must be able to lift the weight as to not injure the lifter during the process.

Living a life pleasing to God will require you to get a spotter. To fulfill your divine assignment you will need a spotter. A spotter will be an individual who will be able to help you lift the heavy weight of the world off your shoulders. The spotter must be spiritually sound, equipped to push you further, and not allow you to settle. The spotter will challenge you beyond your capacity but will know your limits. The spotter cannot be easily distracted. The spotter must pay attention to your details and be wise enough to speak at the appropriate time. The spotter cannot give in easily. Your spotter cannot operate in judgment and must be able to pick up nonverbal clues. Your spotter must have discernment.

As Jesus was carrying the cross to Calvary the Roman soldiers called Simon of Cyrene to help him. The original reason to get him some help may not have been because they were concerned about him. It may have been another form of mockery by saying, "If you think you are the Messiah, why are you so weak and need help?"

Everything they did that fateful day was to mock our Jesus. They put a robe on him to represent him being the Messiah. A crown of thorns was placed on his head as a symbol of him being a king. They took him on a walk of shame carrying the old rugged cross. The cross represented us and our sins as he became our Redeemer. The cross on that day was Jesus' heavy weight. As they walked Jesus through the streets of Jerusalem they felt powerful and in control, but they did not understand he was fulfilling prophesy. Jesus was born to die! In spite of all their wickedness, mockery, and abuse they still did not have the power to take his life. He was on assignment to lay it down.

Simon of Cyrene was in the right place at the right time. There was never a reference he and Jesus knew each other before this encounter, but he was chosen to help. Your spotter may not be your friend you have known for many years. Your spotter needs to operate in wisdom and not familiarity. Your spotter needs to be able to allow the focus to be on you and not be an attention seeker. Your spotter needs to be able to intercede in prayer on your behalf. Everyone cannot be your spotter.

Your friends are valuable to you and may hold a special place in your heart, but a spotter as a specific role. Do not set yourself up for failure by trying to get a friend to fill a role they are not equipped to handle. You will have friends who are simply for a good time. The good time friends are fun to hang with, but may not be the one who carries the anointing of God.

You may have friends for business. Your business friends will help you make career moves, but they may not be the ones you confide in with your personal problems. You will have friends who will be your sounding board. You can tell them your problems and receive wisdom without judgment, but you cannot have a good time with them.

Finally, you will have some spiritual friends. These are the friends you can call at any time to war in the spirit on your behalf. These are the friends that make the enemy tremble when they call on the name of Jesus. Your spiritual friends may be great for intercessory prayer, but not for business. Some friends may play multiple roles in your life, but most will not. If you have a friend that can be all of that to you, then you have a special jewel. Make sure you cherish him/her.

As you evaluate the strengths and weaknesses of your friend circle, you will need to find a spotter. Do not be alarmed if you need to look beyond the friend circle and branch out to someone with power and anointing that can help you carry heavy spiritual weight. A spotter needs to be able to rack the weight and get it off of you at the right time. When you are weak and need someone to help you lift the weight, it is the spotter who will prove to be a great asset. The spotter will lift you up when you are broken. Every woman needs a spotter. Find you a spotter and have him/her in place before you really need them. If you ever get to a point of not being able to lift the weight yourself, your spotter must already be in position. If your spotter is not in position at the right time, then you are subject to injury.

Just as Jesus had Simon of Cyrene you will need a spotter. It might not be your ride or die. I hate to disappoint you, but most people will ride, but will not die. Jesus died for you and he had help from Simon of Cyrene getting to Golgotha. You are trying to get to him and I am sure there is a spotter in the midst just for you.

Choose wisely!

LIFE APPLICATION CHAPTER 6

1. Pray to God to acknowledge that you need some help with your heavy weight
2. Carefully select a spotter (It may not be a close friend)
3. Know when to express that you cannot handle the weight by yourself
4. Do not put more on your friends than they are spiritually equipped to handle

> *Proverbs 16:3 (KJV) "Commit to the Lord whatever you do, and he will establish your plans."*

Personal Goal (Examine yourself and write down what you plan to do differently regarding using a spotter.)

_____
_____
_____
_____
_____
_____
_____
_____
_____
_____
_____

CHAPTER 7

LEARNING TO SAY NO, DENYING SELF TO GLORIFY GOD

Pray for Understanding
Daily Quote:
Saying "no" is necessary sometimes

Message:

Titus 2:11-13 (NIV) "For the grace of God has appeared that offers salvation to all people. It teaches us to say "No" to ungodliness and worldly passions, and to live self-controlled, upright and godly lives in this present age, while we wait for the blessed hope—the appearing of the glory of our great God and Savior, Jesus Christ."

Women spend so much time caring for and nurturing others that we often allow our spirit to become weakened. We give and give of ourselves until we have nothing left for us. We sacrifice, we settle, and sometimes we say yes when we know it is in our best interest to say "no." We sometimes attach love and respect to the need to say "yes" even when we do not get that same love and respect reciprocated. We say yes to prove we love others and believe that a simple "no" means we are being inconsiderate. Saying "no" is not selfish. Sometimes it is absolutely necessary for self-care and recognition of self-worth.

Read Titus 2 in your spare time. It teaches the elders how they should relate to the younger generation and it teaches us how we should govern ourselves and turn away from unrighteousness to live self-controlled lives. To practice self-control, one must be able and willing to say "no". Learning to say "no" is not a bad thing. It is bad when we say yes and suffer grave consequences. It is bad when we say yes and our needs go unmet, then we spend hours murmuring and complaining. It is time to say no and be healthy.

"Saying No To Self!": We are made up of body, soul, and spirit. Your body is your physical being, your soul is your mind, and your spirit is God's connection, direction, and protection. Your spirit belongs to God. We have a choice to present our body and mind to him, but the spirit is his.

We are in a constant battle between our flesh (body and mind) and the spirit. The ability to say "no" to yourself takes will power. Saying "no" to self is choosing to allow your spirit to be in control. You must think before you react to recognize no is a viable option. We become trapped in so many sinful situations which test our ability to say "no" to self. The enemy wants to destroy you by forcing you to destroy yourself. He uses your "yes to the flesh" to turn you away from God. Everything begins in the mind before it is executed. You think in sin, then you react!!

The enemy sets the perfect trap. Do you ever wonder why the trap looks just like you like, smells like you like, walks as you like, says what you like, tastes as you like and shows up at the perfect time? Satan knows your weaknesses because at some point you have spoken it into the atmosphere. Stop giving him the fuel to ignite your fire!

The flesh always desires what it cannot have. Do you think Adam and Eve were concerned about the fruit? They were attracted to what they could not have. Greed started in the garden. Pleasing the flesh feels sooooooo good until it is time to face the consequences and spiritual conviction. Conviction is an indication of your connection to God! If you do not face conviction then you should worry.

It is time to assess your life and learn to live a controlled life as referenced in the book of Titus. To give God your best you must say no to yourself. God will not force his way on you, but he will get you to do what he needs from you at the right time. He will place your back against the wall and place you in a state of surrendering when he has seen enough self-destruction. Say "no" to self is denial! Self-denial takes self-control. Say no to self and watch God move greatly in your life. Saying no to self is saying yes to God.

Saying no to self is maturation and growth. Tell your flesh no and walk in God's presence. It WILL be lonely, painful sometimes, and you will be misunderstood, but God will be glorified. THE REWARD FOR YOUR OBEDIENCE IS OUT OF THIS WORLD!

Matthew 16:24 (KJV) "Then Jesus said to his disciples: If any man will come after me, let him deny himself, and take up his cross, and follow me."

"Saying No To Him": Well, well, well! This one right here. Remember ladies The Girl Code is about empowering women to live our lives according to biblical principles for godliness. It will never be about male bashing. We were created to be a helpmeet to man, but man can be the very reason we cannot live righteous, godly, upright lives. Once we connect ourselves to the wrong one it is hard to pull away. If you discern that you are not right for him learn to say "no". The man is not the problem. The problem is we said yes instead of saying "no".

Titus 2:12 tells us that we should turn from godless living and sinful pleasures. We should live in this world with wisdom, righteousness, and devotion to God. Saying yes to inappropriate late night calls, texts and direct messages generally contradicts our devotion to God. Saying yes to advances from someone else's husband is unrighteousness. Saying yes to a man that is not your husband, if you are married and he is single is not righteous. Saying yes to the guy who you discern is not who God has chosen for you is not wise. We love God and want to please him, but "he" (the nice looking fella) is irresistible. If your spirits do not connect, learn to say "no." Do not follow his words because the enemy is cunning and will know exactly what to say. Connecting in the flesh does not mean God has ordained the union.

When the lights go off the flesh can be easily satisfied, but what happens when the enemy attacks can the two of you war against the devil ***together.*** We should not desire to live in this world without companionship, but being linked to the wrong person is damaging to your mind, body, and spirit. Just think where you might be if you had said "no" to the one who caused you the most pain.

SIDE NOTE: This lesson is talking about illicit relationships which were not ordained by God and it is not talking about marriage. Marriage is honorable in the sight of God, but the problem with marriage is one or both have decided to say "NO" to doing things God's way. Failed marriages are because one or both said no to God and said yes to self. A three-stranded cord is not easily broken (husband, God, wife). God should be the center of marriage. God is the marriage mediator and without him, the fight continues. Saying "no" in marriage should be after consulting God.

Saying "no" to him (the nice guy who wants your attention, but does not want your anointing) is what we are talking about. Ladies, it is time to start saying "no". Everyone who thinks you are pretty is not worthy of a position. Everyone who gives you a flattering compliment is not fit for a connection. Practice the art of accepting the gesture without giving the goods. Stop settling for less because he made you smile. Smile pretty, walk boldly, and when asked to go further say, "NO!" Govern yourself by the Holy Spirit and not by the spirits (wine, vodka, tequila, etc.)

Women, value yourselves. Your phone number is valuable because it gives a man a connection to you. Your email is valuable because it opens up your world to someone else. Befriending someone on social media is valuable because you have given surveillance of your life to another and invited him into your private messenger. Place value on everything that is yours. You are fearfully and wonderfully made! Learn to smile pretty and say, "No, thank you!"

Dating can be fun and pleasurable to some yet daunting to others. Knowing when to exercise the power of "no" is key! Enjoy life, but live according to God's will for your life. God is watching you because you belong to him. Say yes to God and resist the devil at all times. The devil will not be red with horns; he will be just what YOU like.

"Saying No To It!": What is "it?" It is the thing, habit, passion, desire, behavior which satisfies you and hinders your mind, body, and spirit from being healthy. Notice I did not say "happy"; happiness is circumstantial and it fluctuates. Being happy is tied to our emotions. Think about it, you can be in a highly festive place with everybody having a great time and you are miserable. The atmosphere can be extremely happy, but if your emotions are not in check, then you cannot experience happiness.

Your "it" also displeases God because it takes your mind from being stayed on him. "It" usually is the thing you hide from your pastor, parents, and prestigious people. "It" is good when it can be hidden, but at the end of the day, it causes you shame or embarrassment.

"It" is personal. No two people have the same "it" because we are wired differently and find pleasures in different things. "It" attaches itself to your mind and even your heart, but causes your spirit to struggle. After you engage in "it" you start questioning yourself. You say things like: why did I, if only I had, I should have, I really did not mean to, or I did not need that! You try to pray for change and strength to resist "it," but you keep yielding into temptation. "Yielding is sin!" Praying for change is synonymous to scheduling the test. You will not know you are changed until "it" shows up and you pass by finally saying "no." Praying for strength is to request more weight. How will you know you are stronger if the weight does not increase? Success is when you can carry more.

Some examples of "it" to help you identify your stronghold are: rude and abusive language, overeating, obsessive shopping, slander of others, jealousy, envy, vulgarity, depression, anxiety, sex, low self-esteem, impulsiveness, greed, drugs, alcohol, trying to fit in to name a few. Your "it" will not have control over you if you learn to say "no." Recognize what your "it" is and say no when it rises up. Practice discipline and self-control!

This one will probably be the biggest challenge because it is easy to blame others, but what do we do when we are to blame! Titus 2:11-13 (Amplified Bible) tells us to reject ungodliness, worldly (immoral) desires and live sensible, upright and Godly lives. This is life with a purpose that reflects spiritual maturity. As you know better you should strive to do better. If you know it displeases God, then you should grow up and work to stop doing it. Say no to "it".

"Saying No To Others": Titus 2:13 tells us all that we are doing to live self-controlled, upright, and godly is because we are waiting for our blessed hope and the appearing of our Great God. Everything we do is to prepare us to see God. It would be a shame to live in hell on earth and spend eternity in hell. What a shame! Sometimes the hell we encounter is not our own battles. Many of us empathize and take on other people's burdens. It is time to "say no to others."

Say "no" to carrying other people's misfortunes as your own. It is good to help others and show agape love but use wisdom. Some people will ask for your help, give it to you, and watch you fight for them alone. You know the sister who is always asking you to pray and she keeps doing the same thing. You are up at night praying and she is sleeping well waiting to do it again when she feels better. How about the friend who is always in crisis but never takes the hours of advice you have given her? Learn to discern people in need from the needy. Needy people are always going from one need to the next and never find true satisfaction. These are the people who do what they desire and beg for what they need. Say "no" to other's problems becoming yours.

Learn to help without being hindered! Learn to walk away and decipher which parts to absorb and which parts to let go. Do not continue to allow selfish people to dump their problems on you. Seek more of God and less of people who are never satisfied. Helping others is one thing, but carrying others is a choice. Self-care is paramount. Exercise the power of "no". Even Jesus told individuals "no" in the Bible when he did not desire to move when they wanted him to. Do not do something and regret it for years to come because you failed to say "no". Saying "no to others" means I value my own position in this matter. You have the right. If someone cannot respect your "no," they are not entitled to your "yes." It is clearly about them! If your "yes" causes you to suffer then say "no"! You cannot be good for others if you are not good for you.

LIFE APPLICATION CHAPTER 7

1. Pray to God for times when you need to say "no"
2. Deny yourself when your "yes" causes you pain and contradicts the word of God
3. Use discernment to choose how to engage others
4. Understand saying "no" is necessary sometimes for self-care

Proverbs 16:3 "Commit to the Lord whatever you do, and he will establish your plans."

Personal Goal (Examine yourself and write down what you plan to do differently regarding saying "no".)

_____
_____
_____
_____
_____
_____
_____
_____
_____
_____
_____

CHAPTER 8

HOW TO LOSE AND NOT BECOME LOST

Pray for Understanding
Daily Quote:
*"I shall not lose myself in what I have lost;
I belong to God who sustains me"*

Message:

John 11:1-4 (KJV) "Now a certain man was sick, named Lazarus, of Bethany, the town of Mary and her sister Martha. (It was that Mary which anointed the Lord with ointment and wiped his feet with her hair, whose brother Lazarus was sick.) Therefore his sisters sent unto him, saying Lord, behold, he whom thou lovest is sick. When Jesus heard that, he said, This sickness is not unto death, but for the glory of God, that the Son of God might be glorified thereby."

For a spiritual reference on experiencing loss, we will use "Lazarus" not so much for the outcome of him being raised from the dead but because the story of Lazarus speaks to the emotional contexts of grief and its stages. This is a familiar passage and many of us know that Lazarus was Jesus' friend who was ill and his sisters Mary and Martha summoned Jesus to come and heal him. However, Jesus did not immediately respond to their call and Lazarus died.

While Jesus knew that Lazarus' sickness would not end in death, the others did not know. When they witnessed the physical death of Lazarus, Mary and Martha along with many others wept and the sisters became angry with Jesus. When Jesus saw their weeping it sorrowed him and "Jesus Wept!" Your weeping breaks Jesus' heart, as a Father, because he loves and cares for you.

Please note that grief is not only associated with death. Grief is associated with any significant loss. Grief can be expressed with any abrupt change in life that causes pain and sorrow. Grief has stages; denial, anger, bargaining, depression, and acceptance.

Denial: An initial stage of grief is to deny within yourself that the separation has happened. One cannot believe that he or she will no longer have the continued presence of the person, thing, object or standard of living (loss of job/resources). The brain knows reality but the heart is not ready to believe it. Denial is a defense mechanism for pain and unpleasant things. One defends the heart from accepting reality in an attempt to internally remove the sting of the pain.

Denial seeks to guard the heart at the initial point of shock. Being in the denial stage is normal but staying there for a prolonged time can bring mental and emotional instability. I can imagine Mary and Martha initially being in denial when Lazarus died because they trusted that his friend Jesus, the Savior, would come and heal him of his illness but it did not happen as they planned. They just couldn't believe their brother died!

Lazarus' death was to be symbolic of Jesus being raised from the dead so the people could witness the power of God. As we cope with separation from others, things, etc. we must hold to our faith that God's will shall be done. Healing does not always come how we think it should come. Healing from pain and sorrow may not come easy but it's necessary. You must not become lost in denial because God is still in control.

Anger: Anger is the next stage of grief we will explore. Anger is defined as a strong feeling of annoyance, displeasure or hostility.

> *Ephesians 4:26 (KJV) says "Be angry, and sin not: let not the sun go down upon your wrath.*

Anger is an emotion that we all feel at times but anger during the grieving process may sometimes be misdirected. You may have less patience and get angry with family and friends during this time because you are hurting.

In the story of Lazarus, Mary and Martha were angry with Jesus because he did not come and save their brother Lazarus from dying. They were hurt and angry. How many of us get angry with Jesus when someone, a situation, marriage, standard of living, etc. dies? We may feel like Lord, I've done exactly what you said to do, I trust you, have faith in you and even prayed continuously to you for a pleasurable outcome and you still let them or it die! This anger is usually the result of truly not believing that God loves us and knows what's best. God loved Lazarus,

Mary, and Martha but he wanted them to experience the glory of him being raised from the dead. They didn't know that!

God loved your love one also and their healing came through the transition. He removed their pain and suffering because he loved them as well. You do not know what they prayed for God to do! Paul says in 2 Corinthians 5:8 to be absent from the body is to be present with the Lord. Those in Christ were prepared for that day and they are not lost. If you think about losing a significant relationship, maybe you had to experience the loss so that God could heal your brokenness.

You were wallowing in prolonged hurt and the separation allowed you to begin to heal. Remember the pain of trying to hold on! If you had to lose a standard of living, remember when your lifestyle changed and you didn't know how you would make it, you focused more on God. Maybe he needed to remove the earthly distractions because you became comfortable in the flesh and did not spend enough time with him.

It is ok to experience some initial anger. Just do not stay stuck there. God knows what is best for you. Maybe the pain of watching the continued decline of a loved one would have been too much to bear. He may have spared you from lengthy hurt. Be comforted in knowing that he will comfort you during your time of sorrow. As you grieve and experience anger, hold on to your faith and hope. God will take care of you. He will never leave you nor forsake you. Trust his plan!

Bargaining: Bargaining during the grief process is trying to clearly understand the dynamics of the separation. Bargaining is the exploration of the "If and then" process. If something would have happened or would not have happened then the outcome would have been different.

Mary and Martha used the bargaining stage when engaging Jesus after Lazarus died. They said to Jesus "If you had been here then my brother would not have died". Lazarus' death was a part of God's plan and it was going to happen regardless of the presence of Jesus. When we deal with grief many of us go through this phase to seek a source of blame or to better understand the circumstances that resulted in the separation. The bargaining stage is a way for us to seek to understand how, when and why it happened. Maybe you find yourself saying "If I would have gone over there then..." "If he or she would have not gone there then..." "If I would have answered the phone then..." "If he or she had gone to the doctor sooner or followed the advice of the doctor then..." "If I had done this or not done that then..." IF THIS IS YOU, STOP IT NOW.

God is the author and finisher of our fate. Trust that the outcome is what God has allowed and the Holy Spirit is there for you as a comforter.

Trust that the outcome is what you must endure at this time. God's will must be done. If you are bargaining over the death of a loved one, then understand that to be absent from the body is to be present with the Lord. If you are bargaining over the demise of a marriage or significant relationship then understand that the hurt you felt during the relationship was being prolonged and separation is a way for your joy and peace to be restored. (Ask yourself, were you really happy? Do you want that actual feeling again? Maybe they didn't see your value and you matter too much to God for him to leave you there?)

If you are bargaining over the loss of wages/resources/material things then understand that seasons change and the change of season is usually initiated by some rain. It may be raining now but cover yourself with the blood of Jesus and walk through the storm. Stop revisiting the moment of heartbreak. Trouble won't last always.

Bargaining traps your mind in a struggle with the unknown. Trust God and if you did all that you could do, then rest easy with the outcome. Don't become lost in bargaining it is a burden of the mind that will not change the outcome.

Depression: Depression is a mood disorder that causes a persistent feeling of sadness and loss of interest and can interfere with your daily functioning.

An example of a great loss in the Bible is Mary and Martha who experienced sadness over the death of their brother Lazarus. The Bible speaks of Lazarus being dead for 4 days, so it's likely that depression was not experienced by his sisters but they were indeed sad. Many of us can relate to the pain of a great loss. Dealing with the aftermath of separation by death, divorce, loss of income, loss of resources and a diminished standard of living may cause one to experience depression.

While sadness is normal, depression is not an emotion which we should associate with lightly. Depression is a mood disorder and if left untreated it can become life-altering. During depression, an individual will experience increased sadness but it may reach elevated levels that negatively impact daily functioning and trigger other symptoms.

A depressed individual may lose interest in previously enjoyed activities and have a loss of appetite or an extreme increase in appetite, experience crying episodes, fatigue and becomes controlled by the emotions associated with thoughts of the traumatic incident. Depression is real and should not be taken lightly.

Depression is one of the stages of grief but depending on the severity of the depressed episode one may need therapeutic intervention and medication maintenance. Depression, if left untreated and uncontrolled, may lead to the onset of other mental illnesses. As we grieve, it's important to remain healthy in the process. To overcome mild depression an individual must consciously seek normality and use coping skills. However, if healthy daily functioning becomes impossible, seek help!

Depression can become major and result in a major restructuring of the mind. Individuals who suffer major depression, often seek ways to numb their emotions by self-medicating with prescription drugs, over the counter medications, drugs, and alcohol, sex or even engage in risky behaviors to cope with their emotional pain.

If you feel depressed, SEEK HELP! Needing a therapist/counselor/social worker is not a sign of being crazy, it's a sign of an identified imbalance in your normal state of functioning. It's recognizing that you are stuck in your crisis and knowing you need someone to help you get through the unknown. A clinical team will assess your specific needs and develop a plan of care just for you. If you don't feel understood by others, I can assure you that your clinical team will work diligently to understand you and guess what, HELP YOU BETTER UNDERSTAND THE HURTING YOU!

Don't get lost in depression you may never find the old you again without the proper help. You will not know the effects of counseling if you never give it a try. What do you have to lose? If you seek help you will place yourself in a position to be free to, once again, live a functioning life as you work to accept your new normal.

Acceptance: Acceptance is coming to terms with reality. It is acknowledging that the separation has happened. Acceptance is realizing that the outcome was to be regardless of how you as an individual hoped it would be. "It happened and I acknowledge that it happened." Acceptance sets you up to move on.

Mary and Martha had accepted that Jesus had the power to heal their brother Lazarus. Then, they accepted that Lazarus was dead since it had been four days but Jesus had another plan. Lazarus was raised from the dead. At the end of the miracle, they accepted that Jesus had the power to raise him up and that is good news! Although we may not experience this in our situations just as Lazarus did, we symbolically go through a period of being raised from the death of brokenness if we accept that Jesus has the power to raise us up too. You may have experienced the traumatic loss and feel hopeless but imagine the voice of God speaking loudly to you right now, calling your name and saying "Come out!" Come out of the hurt and pain. You shall live! If he did it before, he can do it again. Activate your faith!

As you accept the outcome of the separation reflect on the role you played, the choices you have made and the things you did or neglected to do. You can't control what has transpired in the past but through prayer and supplication, you can seek God for your future. Separation is not always a bad thing but it can hurt.

No longer having the daily presence of a loved one is painful but watching one suffer in sickness is just as painful. If your loved one died in Christ he/she is not lost, they have transitioned to glory. "No more pain!" If you have not accepted the breakup/divorce be encouraged that God honors marriage but Satan hates it so the attack of the enemy had to be great for the believers. Satan didn't win, God removed your suffering. If the marital covenant (vows) were broken then the covenant was null and void ANYWAY!

If you have not accepted the loss of a job/resources strategically plan a new path for your life and get another job. If you have lost your home or business, partner with someone who can guide you through the process so that you will not make the same mistakes twice. Next time you will be operating from a posture of wisdom.

Acceptance in the grief process is the ultimate goal but it takes perseverance. You must endure the other stages if they present themselves to get to acceptance. Acceptance is deliverance from the pain. Acceptance is a reflection of your healing. If you have not gotten to the stage of acceptance don't be hard on yourself just don't lose hope. Grief is a process! Accept that God loves you and accept that you love yourself enough to keep living.

Don't get so lost in death that you die as well! Don't get so lost in divorce or the loss of a friend that you wound yourself and everything and everyone you come in contact with? Don't get so lost in lack of resources that you can't handle the things within your control. Don't get so lost in grief that you forget to count your blessings! Accept your new normal and allow the Lord to comfort you. My sister, COME OUT! God is calling you just as he called Lazarus. You shall live and not die!

LIFE APPLICATION CHAPTER 8

1. Pray to God to ask him to be your comforter
2. Seek to understand your role in the process, you've done your best, give the rest to God
3. Pray for acceptance of God's will for your life and the life of others
4. Acknowledge that some loses are necessary for your protection.

Proverbs 16:3 "Commit to the Lord whatever you do, and he will establish your plans."

Personal Goal (Examine yourself and write down what you plan to do differently regarding grief.)

_____
_____
_____
_____
_____
_____
_____
_____
_____
_____
_____
_____

CHAPTER 9

KNOW YOUR ISSUE SO YOU CAN BE HEALED

Pray for Understanding
Daily Quote:
"My issue does not define me for I am healed"

Message:

Mark 5: 25-34 (NLT) "A woman in the crowd had suffered for twelve years with constant bleeding. She had suffered a great deal from many doctors, and over the years she had spent everything she had to pay them, but she had gotten no better. In fact, she had gotten worse. She had heard about Jesus, so she came up behind him through the crowd and touched his robe. For she thought to herself, "If I can just touch his robe, I will be healed." Immediately the bleeding stopped, and she could feel in her body that she had been healed of her terrible condition. Jesus realized at once that healing power had gone out from him, so he turned around in the crowd and asked, "Who touched my robe?" His disciples said to him, "Look at this crowd pressing around you. How can you ask, 'Who touched me?'" But he kept on looking around to see who had done it. Then the frightened woman, trembling at the realization of what had happened to her, came and fell to her knees in front of him and told him what she had done. And he said to her, 'Daughter, your faith has made you well. Go in peace. Your suffering is over.' "

SHE KNEW HER ISSUE, DO YOU KNOW YOURS? This passage of scripture deals with the woman with the issue of blood. This woman had been plagued with the issue of blood for twelve years. She had spent all of her money on doctors trying to rid herself of the issue. One day she heard that Jesus was in town and she had enough faith and determination to know that if she could just touch the hem of his garment she would be made whole. Being made whole is different from being healed. Wholeness is a complete restoration without any remnants left behind. Being returned to the original state.

Jesus was en route to Jarius' house because Jarius' daughter was sick and was about to die. Jarius, the synagogue ruler, wanted Jesus to go to his house and touch his daughter because he believed Jesus' healing was in the touch. It was uncommon for a synagogue ruler in all his power to believe in the power of Jesus and he didn't believe that Jesus could heal her with speaking the words, Jarius' faith was in the touch. Regardless of when, where and how long you have your issue, Jesus can make you whole, if you believe.

The Bible tells us that the woman had the issue of blood for 12 years. Because it never stated that she was twelve years old and she was referred to as a woman, we can determine that at one time in her life she was considered normal. Unfortunately, some women are born into their issues.

The word issue is mentioned 38 times in the KJV bible. For the sake of time, I will name a few:

*Genesis 48:6 states, and **thy issue**, which thou begettest after them, shall be thine, and shall be called after the name of their brethren in their inheritance.*

*Leviticus 15:2 states, Speak unto the children of Israel, and say unto them, When any man hath a **running issue** out of his flesh, because of his issue he is unclean.*

*Leviticus 15:3 states, and this shall be his uncleanness in **his issue**: whether his flesh run with his issue, or his flesh be stopped from his issue, it is his uncleanness.*

Number 5:2 Command the children of Israel that they put out of the camp every leper, and every one that hath an issue, and whosoever is defiled by the dead:

Proverbs 4:23 Keep thy heart with all diligence; for out of it are the issues of life.

*Matthew 22:25 Now there were with us seven brethren: and the first, when he had married a wife, deceased, and having **no issue**, left his wife unto his brother*

In these scriptures, the referenced issues were not clearly identified, we read thy issue, running issue, his issue, an issue, the issue, and no issue. Unlike, that of the woman with the issue of blood. Her issue was clearly identified. It was made known what her issue was and she was the one that was made whole. Identify your issue and God can make you whole.

Every time we read of an issue in the bible we read of uncleanliness. As long as the issue existed there was uncleanliness and a need for isolation. As long as we as believers have unresolved issues, we can sometimes be subjected to a poisoning of the mind, body, spirit and it often leads to moments of isolation and turmoil. Having an issue is not the totality of our problem. It is when we don't do anything to move beyond the contaminant. I'm sure the woman with the issue of blood wanted to give up on many occasions. Especially, as she spent all her money on doctors and doctor's opinions and she kept getting worse.

But God! Because of her determination to keep trying to find a cure, we know she felt that this issue was not until death. Change comes when we: identify the issue, accept the issue and bring the issue to God.

As humans, it is hard to find fault and issues within ourselves. You are the product of your parent's morals, values, and other environmental influences. How you process and interpret things is what may cause an issue for you in certain situations.

Start trying to identify your own issues so that you can be a better steward in the body of Christ and remove relationship barriers. Unresolved issues may be poisoning your personal engagements with others. You find yourself able to hide in crowds by masking your pain with laughter but once you get personal with someone and your issues are exposed you cannot handle someone pressing on the unhealed wound.

The woman with the issue of blood did not make a spectacle of herself. She did not need to be brought to Jesus in some ceremonial fashion, she just needed to touch his garment. She needed determination and faith. This woman knew where to go for healing. When all else failed Jesus was the answer. When we deal with issues, Jesus is still the answer. We must take our issues to him and believe that he can make us whole. All of us have some type of issue.

All issues are not till death but we must trust and believe that. Remember, Job had issues but he continued to trust and worship God in spite of his circumstances. Too many of us give up on God and church the moment we can't handle our issue. When was the last time you went to Jesus with your issue? I am not speaking of a problem with a solution. Truth be told, you know what you must do to solve your problem but it may not be favorable or cause pain so you avoid making the best decision for you. I am talking about a life-altering issue. Problems are temporary and usually based on some condition or choice that we have or have not made. Issues cause you to be unclean in your mind, heart and physical being.

When was the last time you really sought God to be made whole of the issue that has you unclean? Have you identified your issue? Have you accepted that you have an issue? And lastly, have you reached earnestly to touch Jesus?

This woman could have prayed and asked for healing, but she needed a special touch. She could have called her priest to pray some more but she needed a special touch. She could have had a crying session with her friends but she needed a special touch. You have got to touch God to become healed. Every time you have a moment to touch him, seek him. You may have to crawl down on your belly as if you are making your way through a crowd. Do not let anything or anyone stand in your way.

This may be the difference between spiritual life and death. Identify your issue, accept that you have an issue, and reach out to God for his touch in your life. Then and only then will you be made whole. The woman with the issue, is all of us! We see that woman, every time we look in the mirror. Common issues that plague women: being spoiled, molestation, rape, lack of resources, relationship pains, being silenced as a child with no voice, low self-esteem, abandonment, rejection, poor body image, jealousy, envy, greed, being selfish, lack of self-respect, abuse, and addictions to name a few. Jesus is waiting to make you whole, what are you waiting for? She knew her issue, do you know yours?

LIFE APPLICATION CHAPTER 9

1. Pray to God to identify your issue
2. Give your issue a specific name, it is not a person
3. Seek God for healing from your issue
4. Believe that your issue can be healed through God

> *Proverbs 16:3 "Commit to the Lord whatever you do, and he will establish your plans."*

Personal Goal (Examine yourself and write down what you plan to do differently regarding identifying your issue and being made whole.)

_____
_____
_____
_____
_____
_____
_____
_____
_____
_____
_____
_____

CHAPTER 10

YOU ARE QUALIFIED TO WORK IN GOD'S KINGDOM

Pray for Understanding
Daily Quote:
"I've Got Work to do in the Kingdom of God and I'm Qualified"

Message:

2 Kings 4:1 (NLT) "One day the widow of a member of the group of prophets came to Elisha and cried out, 'My husband who served you is dead, and you know how he feared the Lord. But now a creditor has come, threatening to take my sons as slaves.' "

This passage of scripture deals with the widow woman coming to Elisha. The reason she was able to go to Elisha was because of the qualifications of her husband. Her husband, at some point in his life, became qualified to be among the group of prophets. He was qualified to serve Elisha. Thus, the significance of the relationship the dead husband had with Elisha. Therefore, it was significant for the woman to explain to Elisha that "my husband who served you is dead". She was not just talking about anybody who didn't matter, she wanted Elisha to know who she was talking about and what he had done while he was living. She also told Elisha "you know how he feared the Lord." She wanted Elisha to know that her husband had done good works and feared God, now he is gone but he left her in debt. He had unfinished business.

Assess your current circle and identify your connections. Who are you connected to? Are you connected to a prophet in a way that others can go to him on your good works? Are you with qualified people who are sent by God to show you what you need to sustain yourself spiritually and in this world? The widow woman teaches you about having the **right connections,** living a life in the **fear of God**, having **unfinished financial business** and **recognizing the value in what you already possess.**

> *2 Kings 4:2 (NLT) "What can I do to help you?" Elisha asked. "Tell me, what do you have in the house?" Nothing at all, except a flask of olive oil," she replied.*

The woman was able to use the flask of olive oil to start her a business of selling oil. She was able to sell the oil to pay the creditors. She even had enough for her and her sons to live off the remainder. The woman was able to immediately go to work because of what she already possessed. You can work in God's Kingdom because of what you already possess.

The Kingdom needs 3B's

The Bold: proclaiming the gospel, teachers, and students of the word, prayer warriors

The Busy: the workers

The Believers: the talkers who will spread the word and get others to join in.

There are no perfect people in the Kingdom but you must be committed and willing to do the work. Jesus didn't have perfect people with him but they left their familiar territories to follow him.

God is looking for the Bold!: Are you bold enough to take a stand like Peter by speaking and teaching the uncompromised word of God? You must be willing to step on a few toes to maintain your integrity and not compromise the Word of God. You must be a strong voice for the people of God. Peter would say what the others would not. He became their mouthpiece and leader.

The Busy: These are the workers like Peter, James, and John. Willing to do more than others and go when no one else is going. The ones who don't mind **going to the meetings** and doing the leg work. The ones who **brainstorm** the ideas and work at the events and functions.

The Believer: You may not be bold or busy but you believe. You are the one who can go out and tell somebody about the Kingdom and the experience of God's grace and mercy. Go out and spread the good news like Andrew, Simon, and Philip.

Doubters like Thomas (naysayer): You might even be a doubter like Thomas who needs proof to believe. It's the naysayers that challenge and force the leader to be stronger.

You are QUALIFIED to work in the Kingdom! You're regular, like the disciples, but you have relevance: Do you like shopping? – There is shopping in the Kingdom. You can be the one who does online research for products and services. Do you like cooking? – There is cooking in the Kingdom, CULINARY MINISTRY! Be the one who cooks for the events. Do you like fashion? – There is a ministry right now looking for the right uniform, you can help. Do you like makeup and cosmetics? – There is a photo shoot scheduled for someone in the Kingdom, become a BEAUTY CONSULTANT and beat the faces of the ministry staff. Do you like cleaning? - Become the church custodian or help with cleaning up after service. Do you just like being left alone with a task? - There are some envelopes that need to be stuffed and copies that need to be made. You can work by yourself.

Do you like dancing? – There is dancing in the Kingdom, help with the liturgical dances or when the music plays get your dance on! Are you nosey and like to tell everybody's business? – Find out what is going on in your church and create a bulletin or newsletter. Then ask the administration if you can read the announcements. Go tell others what is going on in your church. Do you like order? – There is a church meeting that will need a Sargent-At-Arms. Do you like talking on the phone? - Join the KEEPER's ministry and call all the new members and personally welcome them to your church. Do you like working with computers and graphics? – Become a member of the media ministry and express yourself.

When you are following the plan that God has for you, things will begin to flow and you will have an overflow. The bible says the widow woman had more than enough. The oil flowed until all the jars were filled and when her son told her that there were not any more jars to be filled the oil stopped flowing. There should be no greed and waste in the Kingdom. God will supply all your needs if you heed to his instructions.

God values you and has gifted you for his glory. You are qualified to work in the Kingdom of God by what you already possess. Transform your mind and use your talents for the Kingdom of God. God is waiting on you, and yes, you are qualified.

LIFE APPLICATION CHAPTER 10

1. Pray to God and tell him yes to working in the Kingdom of God
2. Identify the talent or gift you want to use in the Kingdom and get to work
3. Identify if you are bold, busy or a believer

Proverbs 16:3 "Commit to the Lord whatever you do, and he will establish your plans."

Personal Goal (Examine yourself and write down what you plan to do differently regarding being qualified to work in the Kingdom of God.)

_____
_____
_____
_____
_____
_____
_____
_____
_____
_____
_____
_____
_____

CHAPTER 11

WHEN YOUR EMOTIONS DON'T MATCH YOUR CHARACTER

Pray for Understanding
Daily Quote:
"Emotions are feelings, Character is who I am"

Message:

John 11:17-35 (NIV) "On his arrival, Jesus found that Lazarus had already been in the tomb for four days. Now Bethany was less than two miles from Jerusalem, and many Jews had come to Martha and Mary to comfort them in the loss of their brother. When Martha heard that Jesus was coming, she went out to meet him, but Mary stayed at home. 'Lord,' Martha said to Jesus, 'if you had been here, my brother would not have died. But I know that even now God will give you whatever you ask.' Jesus said to her, 'Your brother will rise again.' Martha answered, 'I know he will rise again in the resurrection at the last day.' Jesus said to her, 'I am the resurrection and the life. The one who believes in me will live, even though they die; [26]and whoever lives by believing in me will never die. Do you believe this?' 'Yes, Lord,' she replied, 'I believe that you are the Messiah, the Son of God, who is to come into the world.' ⁸After she had said this, she went back and called her sister Mary aside. 'The Teacher is here,' she said, 'and is asking for you.' When Mary heard this, she got up quickly and went to him. Now Jesus had not yet entered the village but was still at the place where Martha had met him. When the Jews who had been with Mary in the house, comforting her, noticed how quickly she got up and went out, they followed her, supposing she was going to the tomb to mourn there. When Mary reached the place where Jesus was and saw him, she fell at his feet and said, 'Lord, if you had been here, my brother would not have died.' When Jesus saw her weeping, and the Jews who had come along with her also weeping, he was deeply moved in spirit and troubled. 'Where have you laid him?' he asked. 'Come and see, Lord,' they replied. Jesus wept."

Women are often viewed as being emotional beings. We tend to be very expressive with our feelings, we cry, we yell, we laugh and sometimes we even laugh and cry at the same time. We are typically emotional. However, some women are void of emotions and while it is highly respected it is generally a learned behavior. Women who are void of emotions typically have endured life's challenges that require self-protection. Disconnected emotions become a defense.

Jesus had several encounters with women in the bible. He was born of a woman, he met the woman at the well, he healed the woman with the issue of blood, he forgave the woman caught in adultery and a woman was the first to see him after the resurrection. The women were *__carriers of the Good News.__*

Women today still have the task of carrying the good news. Most churches have more women parishioners than men and we pack a mighty punch when it comes to setting the tone and the atmosphere. When a woman is sick the whole house suffers. When the woman is mad there's tension in the land. Being able to control our emotions is pivotal to the welfare of our families, friends and any place we go. Our emotions are what drives us or drives us astray.

Understanding Character

John 11 takes place in Bethany (a small village east of Jerusalem just over the Mount of Olives) and it deals with the death of Lazarus (Jesus' friend) and the emotions of his sisters (Mary and Martha), the people and even Jesus himself. Because verse 35, the shortest verse in the bible reads then "Jesus wept", this lets us know that even Jesus was overcome with emotions.

However, this is not the first time that Jesus has had a personal encounter with Mary and Martha. According to the scriptures, they actually have three encounters but this is the one that stands out above the rest because Lazarus being raised from the dead foreshadowed Jesus' Death and Resurrection because in John 11:4 Jesus said:

John 11:4 (NLT) "Lazarus' sickness will not end in death. No, it happened for the glory of God so that the Son of God will receive glory from this"

3 Separate Encounters with 3 Different Sets of Emotions

ized text *The first was tension between the two sisters over roles:* While Jesus was at their home Mary sat at the feet of Jesus hearing the word and Martha was cooking. Martha was angry because she was working and Mary was not. Martha even told Jesus to tell her to help me and Jesus rebuked her because she was only worried about cooking and Mary chose to hear the word which to him was more important. Both women could have been guilty of being selfish by wanting what she wanted. They were both in their emotions. Martha was feeling angry and used. Mary was feeling intrigued and attentive to Jesus.

The second was grief at the death of their brother Lazarus: Mary believed in Jesus but knowing that he had the power to stop her brother's death and he didn't, made her emotional. She was overcome with emotions and didn't have a problem telling Jesus; Lord, if only you had been here, my brother would not have died. Martha was bold enough to go to him and Mary waited until she was called. Martha even acknowledged that she always believed he was the Messiah but she too felt that if he would have been there her brother would not have died. She was in her emotional grief but her character believed in the power of Jesus. She even had some doubt at this point that Lazarus could be raised from the dead after being dead so long. Their emotions did not reflect their character.

In this scripture, even Jesus became emotional when he saw and heard the crying of the people. He became angry and deeply saddened.

Jesus, never he doubted his ability but he was human and emotional. Our Jesus' emotions at this time didn't reflect his character.

The third encounter was the anointing of Jesus by Mary: Mary poured the expensive perfume to show honor to Jesus. Mary was overcome with gratitude and felt that he was worthy of such an honor. Mary was happy at this moment and her emotions varied from the previous encounters. Emotions are just expressed feelings. We must learn to control our emotions because we don't want to make emotional decisions and come out of character. Making emotional decisions can be very unhealthy and open you up to undue hardship. If you l ead with your emotions you may destroy people, relationships and opportunities with your mouth. Being controlled by your emotions may cause you to behave in a manner to the point where you do not even recognize yourself. What if Jesus had not raised Lazarus because of how Mary and Martha greeted him while in their emotions? We see here 3 encounters with the same people and different emotions exhibited.

1. IDENTIFY WITH YOUR EMOTIONS
2. Don't make emotional decisions (pray and seek God on what you need to do) **IF YOU CANNOT PRAY, PAUSE!**
3. Learn coping skills to combat emotional instability so that you can maintain control
4. Don't get so wrapped up in what others are doing or not doing that you cause God to rebuke you. Stay on your own course.
5. KNOW THAT your emotions are feelings and your character is who you are.

Your emotions will take you places you don't want to go and make you stay longer than you want to stay.

Your character should be connected to God then and only then will the Holy Spirit keep you in check.

LIFE APPLICATION CHAPTER 11

1. Pray to God and repent for emotional outbursts and emotional reactions
2. Write down things that truly describe your character and strive to live by them
3. Reevaluate situations using facts of the engagements, when your character is being tested
4. Write down 5 emotions you admire and incorporate them in your daily life

> *Proverbs 16:3 "Commit to the Lord whatever you do, and he will establish your plans."*

Personal Goal (Examine yourself and write down what you plan to do differently regarding choosing your character over your emotions.)

_____
_____
_____
_____
_____
_____
_____
_____
_____
_____

THE NEED FOR THE CODE

The Girl Code teaches women to remove the layers of unpleasant life experiences to walk in the knowledge of who God uniquely created the woman to be. Application of *The Girl Code* principles is a process of freedom. As you examine yourself and identify who you are in Christ, you will begin to see areas of **YOU** that are in need of readjusting. You will begin to see how your choices and your perceptions of yourself and others are the driving force of your character. You are who you think you are. You can do what you think you can do. There will no longer be a need for envy or comparisons because you will be too satisfied with who you are and who God created you to be.

Knowing The Word of God and applying it to your life are two different things. While you may know The Word and its contexts, if you desire to live for Christ, you must apply it. Without application, you are behaving as a person who lacks a sense of judgment. Many women know The Word and some have the ability to quote scriptures from memory but still struggle with application. The Girl Code is the biblical system to

Godliness by working on you. This code teaches women the principles of self-love and how to live a life pleasing to God first and then self. The principles of this code apply to all women regardless of age, race, status or life experiences. Applying the code will enable you to be free to love yourself in your raw state. This is the period when you are alone without the makeup, weave, lashes, designer clothing, glitz, glam and mask. You won't have to hide what has been healed! You will begin to look in the mirror and be proud of who you have become because you will no longer be captive in your own mind. You will fall deeply in love with your soul and character. You will no longer feel compelled to engage in shameful activities for acceptance or inclusion. You will desire companionship but not yearn for validation. You will become your own stamp of approval.

To begin to love yourself follow the code:

Pray: (*communicate with God*)

Wait On God After You Have Prayed: (*take a time out and wait for the instructions on what to do next*)

Forgiveness: (*forgive God, yourself, others and ask others to forgive you*)

Know Your Role as a Woman: (*operate in order*)

Get a Spiritual Makeover: (*allow God to make you over*)

Get You a Spotter: (*choose a wise person to help you lift the weight when you cannot do it by yourself*)

Learn to Say No: (*deny self and reject the ill intentions of others so you can be healthy*)

Lose and Not Become Lost: (*understand separation and prepare for your new normal*)

Know Your Issue: (*remove the layers and get to the core of your internal struggle(s).*

You Are Qualified to Work in God's Kingdom: (*get to work in the Kingdom by using your gifts*)

Control Your Emotions: (*emotions are feelings, character is who you are*)

Apply the code to your life and walk into your God-Given Authority. In order for this to work you must prepare for a period of separation from distractions. It may seem uncomfortable at first but when you return, you will be a mighty force with a renewed mind. Stop blaming others and work on you. You might not like what you see. Spend more quality time with God in prayer and the Word. I guarantee, you will no longer be the same.

FINAL WORD

"*The Girl Code*" walks women through the biblical system to Godliness. All women are created uniquely by God but most fail to reach fullness in self-love. You are God's masterpiece. Many know the prayer of Salvation but endeavor to live according to God's word. To be saved is to confess with your mouth and believe in your heart that Jesus Christ died for the remission of sins, was buried and is coming back again. The question is, will he know you when he returns by your deeds, actions and works while here on earth? These are things you did when you had free will. What are you choosing to do? Is God pleased? Are you pleased without any shame? Waiting on tomorrow to make a change may be too late. The time is now to transform your life.

Matthew 25:13 (KJV) "Watch therefore, for ye know neither the day nor the hour wherein the Son of man cometh."

This system, *"The Girl Code"*, was inspired by The Word of God through prayer, personal experiences, self-awareness, and observations of others using sound doctrine and a social perspective. So many women seek to change the things they identify as the problem without getting to the core of their struggles. Ask yourself, why do I have a problem with it? What has happened in my life, positive or negative, that has formed my view on things? It is time to uproot layers of pain, guilt, jealousy, disappointment, rejection, low self-image, addiction, hurt and shame. It is time to repair your heart and mind. You cannot repair what you cannot identify as being broken. Problems do not begin on the surface they are simply manifested by our viewpoint on personal experiences.

As I prayerfully seek God on ways to be effective in the Kingdom, I am constantly reminded to remove judgment and to understand that we are the products of our systems (family, school, community, industry and culture) whether good or bad.

Ephesians 6:12 (KJV). "For we wrestle not against flesh and blood, but against principalities, against power, against rulers of the darkness of this world, against spiritual wickedness in high places."

Conflicts are often the result of unresolved internal struggles compounded by life experiences which the enemy uses to redefine our character. These conflicts affect one's cognitive dissonance and are projected onto others as a defense. As women go through life as helpers, many battle to identify the core of their existence. Women work tirelessly to help others while they are hurt. Women inadvertently become the wounded healers.

Most women can identify one or more areas of their life which they are not pleased with but instead of working to develop holistic love for themselves they mask it with more socially acceptable things (make-up, clothes, material possessions, alcohol consumption and careers). To live a life that is pleasing to God, a woman must engage in self-evaluation, repent, deny self and turn from her sinful and wicked ways that keep her in spiritual bondage. *The Girl Code* teaches the principals of self-love in God. You will not have to hide what no longer exists. Deliverance in the Name of Jesus! **If you transform your mind, your character will transform.**

Made in the USA
Columbia, SC
26 June 2025